LAST MEAL AT MOOR INN

By

Nigel Miller

"Jane! You haven't done anything wrong, have you?"

"Mum! Of course not. Why?"

"I only rang because this letter came for you. It's from Grant Bayley, Solicitors of Morecambe."

"I've never heard of them; I don't know why they've written to me."

"Shall I post it on to you?"

"No, I'll come for the day on Sunday."

Why should those solicitors have written to her? With what did she associate firms of Solicitors? Property transactions? She wasn't currently buying or selling a house. Divorces? She was single and didn't know anyone who had matrimonial problems. Defending people in court? She wasn't in trouble with the police and knew nobody who might be. She had rarely visited Morecambe, had no connection with it and knew no one who lived in that area. Had they written to her in error? If so, how had they got to know her home address? She had once met someone who worked for a detective agency and he told her he could get to know her name and address within twenty four hours. She might think nobody could trace her but certain people had their methods. Fortunately it had been a friendly discussion. She decided not to mention the matter to any of her friends in case she did have a problem.

"We thought you weren't going home until the week after next," said her young friend, Danielle.

"Mum rang the other day, so I said I would go for the day on Sunday."

The journey seemed to take longer than usual. All the time she asked herself what could the solicitors have written to her about. She could barely avoid the temptation to speed. Yet after all there might be a simple explanation.

"Here it is." Her mother handed her an envelope which she opened.

" 'We are acting in the administration of Ellen Lavinia Groom.' I've never heard of her. She isn't a distant relative, is she?"

"No. We've never heard of her and we've no one with the name Groom in our family."

"They've sent me a copy of her will. She leaves her estate to be divided equally among the following in recognition of their kindness: Betty Myers, my home help, Norman Price, the landlord of Moor Inn, High Wood, Audrey Price, his wife. I've never heard of Moor Inn. Thomas Carter of Sandton, South Africa, Nora Carter, his wife, Simon Richards of Toronto, Canada, Susan Richards, his wife, Liam, his son, Sally, his daughter, Amanda, his daughter, Jane Carberry of Nottingham, Reginald Boles of Mablethorpe, Lawrence Harvey of Shrewsbury and Beatrice Harvey, his wife. I've never heard of any of them either."

"It's not someone's idea of a joke, is it?" queried her father.

"A firm of solicitors wouldn't be involved in a joke like that," said her mother. "If a private individual had sent this letter then it might be a joke."

"The solicitor says he'll write to me in due course but I would like to find out more."

"Why don't you go and see him."

"Yes, I will do."

"There's something I find a bit difficult to understand," said her father.

"What's that?"

"Your home address is stated in the will: so Ellen Lavinia Groom must have made it before you left home, yet she seems to have known you but not known us. You didn't have any clandestine relationships, did you?"

"No, I didn't and I've got no idea why she should have known me but not known you."

"I am worried about her reasons for leaving her estate to strangers," said her mother. "It may be because of family trouble and I would rather you weren't involved."

"I suppose the family gathered round for the reading of the will."

"That happens in T V serials about wealthy families and in drawing room dramas. It's not like that in real life."

Years ago Jane had overheard her parents talking about the will of a distant relative. A row broke out about to whom she had left her money and greed had torn the family apart. She had not thought much about it at the time and had forgotten all about it until now. Someone had only been left two houses that were not fit for human habitation. The cost of repairing them was more than they were worth and he didn't want them. Jane recalled no names, apart from the two houses no details of the assets, nor what happened afterwards. Like her mother she didn't want to become part of a family row; she wouldn't know how to handle the situation. She was reluctant to ask her parents' advice as she wasn't supposed to have been listening.

She was relieved when her mother changed the subject and she enjoyed a pleasant day at home. As soon as she returned to Liverpool she arranged an appointment with the solicitor. She still refrained from mentioning the will. She had promised to take her three young friends out and decided to take them with her but not to tell her what it was all about.

"I've got to see someone at this firm." Jane stopped her car outside the solicitors' offices. "I won't be long, so don't go far away."

"I only acted for Miss Groom in drawing up her will," Mr Grant explained. "I believe she had some relatives but there was some family trouble. I didn't ask as people usually don't want to talk about it."

"Is there any way I can find out anything?"

"I'm not sure." Mr Grant pondered. "She became friendly with her home help and they used to talk. Miss Myers has retired now but I think she would like a visit from you."

"I've got three younger people with me. Would it be all right if they came?"

"I don't think she'll mind as long as they behave themselves."

"Are you all right?" Jane had expected the three children to be exploring the area but they were standing outside the offices reassuring each other.

"That man came up, offered us some sweets and asked us if we would like to go round the fairground with him: so we walked away."

Jane eyed a man who was disappearing round the corner. "I knew you would have the sense to walk away."

She went to the retirement bungalow where Miss Myers lived. She decided not to go in with the children but asked them to stay nearby. She trusted them to act sensibly if anyone else approached them.

"Do come in." Miss Myers showed Jane into the living room; the furniture was old fashioned but well cleaned and polished. "Take a seat. I'll make a pot of tea and I've got some delicious cakes my niece made."

She suspected Miss Myers was lonely and someone calling was the main event of the day. If she allowed herself to settle down to tea and cakes she would never be able to tear herself away.

"That's very kind of you but I've got three children with me."

"They can come in. I've some orange juice they can have."

Jane glanced out of the window; the children weren't in sight. Thank goodness she couldn't call them in. They might enjoy the orange juice and cakes but afterwards a long drawn out conversation would make them impatient and fractious; they would rather be in the open air. They were too young to understand how much it meant to an older person to have company. She recalled how exasperated she had been at their age when her grandparents called on an elderly couple. The conversation dragged on; she wasn't the least bit interested and fidgeted. When they did leave she overheard the couple comment on her appalling manners. She couldn't understand their predicament but neither could they understand hers. Perhaps her grandparents had been wrong to take her with them. Anyway she didn't want Miss Myers and her three friends to be embroiled in the same problem. She told her about her reaction to the will.

"Ellen didn't talk much about her family but I believe she inherited some money from her parents. Then her brother was killed; he was unmarried and she inherited his money. Their deaths were a shock to her and she was vulnerable. A cousin said he would invest her monies for her. He made a lot of risky investments and she lost most of her money. He said she asked him to invest the monies but she said he didn't ask her; he just did it. Anyway she ended up with little money and nowhere to live: so she had to go round staying with her cousins. In the end they said they couldn't have her anymore; she ended up homeless and was housed in Morecambe."

"That wasn't very nice of them."

"I suppose it wasn't but I don't think she was an easy person to live with and it can be difficult for people with a family to take in an elderly relative."

Jane queried the beneficiaries in the will.

"Ellen did say she didn't want her cousins to have anything but would see I was all right. I didn't know about you or any of the others until I saw a copy of the will. I thought you were people she got to know over the years and corresponded with. I only saw her twice a week and thought you might have visited her on another day."

"Wouldn't she have told you if anyone had visited her?"

"Not necessarily."

"You wouldn't have any idea how she got to know the others, would you?"

"I can't think of anything. I once did hear of an old lady who fell out with her family and got names of people out of the telephone directory to leave everything to."

"My name isn't in the telephone directory."

"Ellen wasn't stupid and wouldn't have done a thing like that. Anyway I can't see how she could get names of people abroad."

"What happened to the other old lady's will?"

"I think members of the family challenged it and had it overturned."

"I'm sorry I can't stay but I've got to find the children."

"It's all right. I may write to some of the others and find out if they knew Ellen."

Jane took her leave and looked for her friends. They weren't too far away and they visited the beach. She raked over in her mind what Mr Grant and Miss Myers had told her. Why shouldn't she write to the other beneficiaries? It might satisfy her curiosity. On the other hand High Wood wasn't very far. It was a desolate place but she had time to travel there and take the children home. She outlined what had happened and they jumped at the prospect of a ride. She studied a map and set off. They soon left the urban areas and travelled onto the high ground; they were absorbed by the sensation of leaving civilisation and all its problems behind.

"That car's been following us." Danielle looked behind. "Perhaps it can't overtake."

"It can," said Danny. "The road's wide enough."

"Why are they following us?"

"They're only enjoying the scenery and looking at things like we're doing, and like the people in the cars that were coming the other way." Jane drove on and they were entranced by the colours and vegetation of the moors and grasslands that melted into the horizon.

"They're right behind us and still following us."

"I'll slow down," said Jane. "So they can go by."

"They've slowed down as well," said Danielle. "There are two people in that car. They are not going to car jack us, are they? Like what happened to a lady last week."

"That kind of thing happens in the cities, not out in the wilds. I'll stop so they can pass."

"Good! They're going by…. Oh, no! They've stopped and are getting out."

Jane and the children locked the doors and wound up the windows.

"Jane, reverse and go round them so they can't car jack us."

"There are four of us, so we can stop them," said Danny.

The man approached. "I'm sorry if we startled you. We had better introduce ourselves; we're Lawrence and Beatrice Harvey. We've been to see Mr Grant, a solicitor, about the will of Ellen Lavinia Groom. We think you may be Jane Carberry."

"Yes, I am."

"Are these children Liam, Sally and Amanda Richards?"

"No, they're not; they're friends of mine."

"We had never heard of Ellen Lavinia Groom before; and we had never heard of you before. One or two of the other names seemed vaguely familiar but we've no idea where we could have met them."

"I hadn't heard of them before."

"We wondered if Mr Grant knew if Mr and Mrs Price were still running Moor Inn but he didn't know them. We thought we would go there and see if we could find out anything. My wife thinks the name is familiar but she can't place it."

"We're on our way there too."

Both parties got going and arrived at an isolated restaurant; it had an air of neglect like premises that were shut down at the end of the holiday season.

"It must be closed," said Mr Harvey. "It's in such an isolated place they couldn't have made it pay."

"I told you we should have rung up first."

"I know you did but the ride was worth it. Now we've got here I think we've been here before but I can't remember when."

Danny pushed at the front door and it opened. He entered and the two girls followed him.

"I don't think he should have gone in," said Mrs Harvey.

"I don't think he should have done but he likes a bit of adventure. We might as well go in; we can say we were looking for a place to have lunch and thought they might be open."

The adults hesitated and then went after the children. The snack bar gave the impression of not being in use but it was intact and the atmosphere made them expect Norman and Audrey Price to walk in and serve them.

"We thought we would have lunch here, but that's not possible."

The children ran round the room and stood at the entrance.

"There are some bungalows over there." Denise pointed.

"Where are you going?" Jane called out.

"To have a look round," replied Danny.

"All right, but don't do any damage."

Mrs Harvey stared after the children. "I remember now: we spent a night here a few years ago. They put people up in those chalets."

"Yes, I remember too." Her husband searched round.

"What are you looking for?"

"The hotel register."

"It's probably been put away but if we found it, it wouldn't help us."

"It might tell us who else had been staying here. I remember having supper in there." He looked into a dining room. The tables and chairs were laid out and the crockery was stacked up in readiness but waiters and customers were lacking.

"I remember having supper in there too," said Jane. "I had forgotten about it but I had only just passed my driving test. I had driven up to Keswick. It was the first time I had been on such a long journey. I got lost and it was late when I ended up here. I phoned Dad and he told me to stay the night. Other people were here but I can't remember them. I don't know if it was the same night as you stayed here."

"We don't recall you and can't remember the date. I can look in my diary when we get home but that doesn't help us now."

"It looks as though we can't contact Mr and Mrs Price so we've come to a dead end in any case. I'm surprised this place has been left unlocked but perhaps it's so remote it won't get vandalised."

"Look at that!" Jane pointed across the grass. "That man approached the children in Morecambe. He must have followed us up here and now he's approached them again."

"We'll help you if he makes any trouble."

"Oh, no. It's not the same man but he looks like him."

The man walked up with the children. "I had better introduce myself. The name's Reginald Boles. I think I know who you are."

They all introduced themselves.

"He thought we might be Liam, Sally and Amanda Richards," said Denise.

"I remember when I stayed here there was a family with three children but these three don't look like a brother and two sisters." He looked at Mrs Harvey. "You said how well behaved they were but the parents said they weren't always like that."

"I don't remember that."

He looked at Jane. "I remember you."

"I don't think I remember you."

"I don't expect you to. I didn't have a girl friend and wanted to speak to you but didn't think I ought to as I might have given you the wrong impression. I thought you must have travelled by bus and wondered whether to offer you a lift the next morning but found you had a car. Anyway if I had you should have refused."

"I had only just passed my driving test and several people said I looked too young."

"It's a pity people of one sex have to feel it's not safe to speak to someone of the other," said Mrs Harvey.

"You shouldn't speak to children either but I only wanted to know who the three were."

"It's also a pity children have to feel it's not safe to speak to adults and vice versa but there it is."

The adults told each other about their reaction to receiving the copy of the will, their contact with the solicitor and what action they had taken. The children embarked on another exploration of the area.

"All those places are locked up," they reported.

"I remember when I came over here for breakfast the old lady was several yards behind me," said Mr Boles. "I turned round and said, 'Good morning' but decided not to say anything else. After breakfast something upset her but I don't know what."

"I remember something about that now," said Mrs Harvey, "but not exactly what."

"I think we've found out everything we're going to find out," said her husband.

They felt a sense of loss in not being able to have a meal there. The isolation created an attraction and a feeling of being far removed from the urban existence and all its troubles. It was an area where children could run wild and be free from harm. Places like that needed to be preserved.

"A couple is speaking to the children. Are they Mr and Mrs Carter or Mr and Mrs Richards?"

"They are too young to be Mr and Mrs Richards," said Mr Boles. "They must be Mr and Mrs Carter."

"No, we're Christopher and Sara Price. Mum and Dad will be here in a minute. Dad's left the place unlocked again. He's not senile but can be forgetful sometimes."

"I remember them now," exclaimed Mrs Harvey as the parents came round the corner. They introduced themselves and shared their experiences.

"We meant to get in touch with the solicitor about the will but never got round to it." Mr Price told them. "We've still got the hotel register." He led them into the office. None of them could recall the exact date. Someone thought it was in one month and someone else thought it was in another month. Mr and Mrs Price were vague about names and dates but eventually they discovered the day and the registration details.

"We see so many people it's difficult to remember," said Mrs Price, "but it's now coming back to me." She turned to Jane. "We thought you were rather young to be travelling alone."

"I remember you serving breakfast in the dining room."

"Let's go in and look round; we may remember some more."

Mr Price unlocked the door and they all filed in.

"The Richards family were sitting by that window as the children wanted to look out," said Mrs Harvey. "They pointed at things. We were sitting behind them with Mr and Mrs Carter."

"I remember being with them but not what we talked about," said her husband.

"You put Miss Groom, Miss Carberry and Mr Boles at separate tables by the wall."

"I think we did. We might have considered putting you three together at one table but an older person doesn't always like being seated with younger people; and putting a young lady with a strange man might have been risky. Seating arrangement can be difficult."

"Yes, I do understand," said Mr Boles. "Did you have a helper at breakfast?"

"No, we always managed to serve breakfast on our own. Miss Groom didn't seem at ease. We thought it must have been because you," Mrs Price looked at Jane, "were on one side of her and you, "she glanced at Mr Boles, "were on the other side and we should have seated her away from her."

"I must have been the first to leave; I eat rather fast. I paid the bill, went to collect my things and came back with the key."

"Then what happened?" asked Jane.

"Miss Groom got up before she finished and asked if she could use the telephone. I told her she could but suggested she should finish her breakfast first."

"I remember that now," said Mrs Harvey. "She did finish her breakfast although she did not seem too happy about it. We finished at the same time as Mr and Mrs Carter and came out to pay the bill. The Richards family were slow with having children. I don't remember where you were still there." She turned to Jane.

"I must have left before you did. I had forgotten about Miss Groom coming along in an awful state saying something about 'They won't have me.'"

"Yes, she did," said Mrs Price, "but I can't remember who else was there."

"It must have happened while I was handing in the key."

"We were all there," said Mr Harvey, "but I don't know about the Richards family."

"The dining room door was open so they must have heard," said his wife.

"I asked her what the matter was," Mrs Price searched her memory. "She didn't have a home and had to stay with relatives but now they couldn't have her and she had nowhere to go."

"I think we all said, 'How awful!' but didn't know what to do about it," said Mr Harvey.

"Mr Richards said the municipal authority would have to house her," said his wife. "I don't know when he joined us. His children weren't with him but he must have told them to stay behind. I'm not sure what happened after that."

"I had to leave but at my age I wouldn't have known what to do," said Mr Boles.

"I had to leave as well as I didn't know what to do either and Dad wanted me to get home as soon as possible."

"What did happen?" asked Mrs Harvey.

"We wondered whether to let her stay here for the time being as she had nowhere else to go, but we were worried about being landed with her. In the end we would have had to ask her to leave but what could we have done if she said she couldn't go? Would we have had to put her in the car and take her to the local authority and dump her? I suppose they would have had to house her, but what would the headlines to the newspapers have been? 'Elderly lady dumped at council offices.' Our names would have been in the papers and it wouldn't have done our business any good."

"It was a terrible situation for anyone to be in," added Mr Price. "We might have let her stay and told the council she needed to be housed but they might have said that while she was here she wasn't homeless."

"In the end Mr Carter said he would take her to the municipality," said Mr Harvey.

"Yes, he did and we let him do that; we didn't know what else to do but he might have been landed with her. We never heard any more until we received the copy of the will. We can only assume he did something to get her housed but what it was we can only guess. I suppose Mr Grant has written to Mr and Mrs Carter in South Africa but doesn't know what they did with her. That will have to remain as one of life's mysteries."

"Yes, it will but at least we know the background. Incidentally we had considered having lunch here but you've obviously closed down."

"We decided to retire as the business had become a rat race and we're getting older."

"What's going to happen to the inn?"

"It's going to be an outdoor centre. I think you would like to use it." Mr Price looked at the three children.

"Yes, we would," they told him.

"Is there anywhere else near here where they serve lunch?"

"The nearest is The Royal Oak but it's 12 miles away. If you don't mind waiting we'll serve lunch. We'll only be too pleased to do it for the last time."

What was Jane to do about her inheritance? She would like to have the money but didn't really need it. She could say she didn't want it like the person who was left the two houses. Thinking back the fact that he had been left them instead of worthwhile assets may have created the family row. She had no idea who would get the money if she didn't accept it; it might go to those whom Miss Groom didn't want to have it. None of the others had mentioned not accepting the money and neither would she.

Christopher and Sara Price went to collect some provisions, their parents prepared lunch and they all ate it together. The nature of human life is such that many events bring strangers together: encounters during journeys, team work in sport, confrontations in the street, and the trauma of natural disasters. A forsaken lady had eked out her lonely existence but in her death had joined people of different ages, classes and backgrounds. They ate and chatted together but all too soon the last meal at Moor Inn reached its end. They intended to meet again but their paths never crossed and Moor Inn entered into oblivion.

DEATH WAS PRESUMED

BY

Nigel Miller

This story and all its characters are fictitious. Any resemblance to persons, living or dead is purely coincidental.

"Perhaps he was murdered."

"Danny! Don't talk like that!" Jane told him.

Denise had told the others that a lady, known as Rosie whom her grandmother used to visit in an old people's home, had died.

"Grandma used to visit her because she never had any other visitors. She couldn't understand why because she was so sweet."

"Didn't she have any relatives?" Danielle had asked.

"Her husband was a steward on a liner. It called at one port and he went missing; they never knew what happened to him. You worked at that home for a while, didn't you? Do you remember her?"

"I didn't work there for very long but I think I remember her and she was a sweet old lady. Your grandmother must be sorry she's died."

"Yes, she is. Rosie used to ask her to buy me presents for my birthdays and Christmas."

"That was kind of her."

"It was. Grandma's going to see if she can visit someone else."

Jane suspected that Danny might want to say more about what might have happened to Rosie's husband and she changed the subject. The children didn't mention him again.

Two days later Jane received a letter from Mary. They had met at a gathering and although they had chatted they hadn't developed any friendship. Mary had started to work for a firm of solicitors. The firm had been instructed to act in the administration of the estates of Rosie and of another resident of the home who was referred to as Mrs Jones. Both ladies written out their wills on a printed will form and Jane had been one of the witnesses. She had forgotten all about that. Mary wondered whether Jane could be of assistance in tracing relatives. She didn't think she could but went to see Mary and told her about Denise's grandmother.

"Yes, I've seen her but she can't tell me any more than the fact that her husband went missing a long time ago. Her son went to Australia on what we would now call a 'gap year' but he didn't keep up with her. Sometimes residents talk to the staff and tell them about families and backgrounds."

"Rosie didn't tell me much. Once she said she hoped her husband would come back to England but I didn't ask her about it. The matron told me about her husband going missing."

"Couldn't she tell you anything? I thought she knew all about it."

"The matron retired because of ill health and died some afterwards. She seems to have been the only one who did know. Perhaps Rosie confided in her but told her not to tell anyone, so she didn't. I thought she might have confided in Denise's grandmother but she said she didn't."

"Young Danny said perhaps he was murdered and I had to tell him off."

"I suppose that could have happened in some countries. One of the assistant solicitors said he might have had a woman in the port; or he might have missed the boat and been stranded there; or he might have been offered a better job and decided to stay there; or he might have had an accident and had no details on him about who he was, so they couldn't contact anyone."

"If he had stayed there wouldn't he have missed his family and his home in England?"

"If his marriage and home life hadn't been happy and he was the type who didn't miss places that wouldn't have mattered to him."

"Where did he go missing?"

"We don't know. The only person who might have known was the former matron. Did Rosie mention her son to you?"

"She said she used to write to him but he didn't reply. She thought something had happened to him but the family wouldn't tell her. Doesn't the home have his address?"

"They do but it's an old one. It's possible he's moved and wrote to tell her his new address but she didn't get his letter or got it and mislaid it."

"I know that does happen. Incidentally what did her will say?"

"As she wrote the will herself it isn't clear but it seems she wanted everything to go to her husband for life and then to her son."

"What about Mrs Jones' will?"

"I don't think you can help with that." Mary hesitated. "I'll tell you in case you can but all clients' business is confidential. You'll promise not to discuss it with anyone, won't you?"

"No, I won't."

"Although she was in the home she wasn't all that old."

"Yes, I remember but she looked old."

"Her family had a history of violent deaths. Her brother was killed in a climbing accident, her husband was killed in a train crash and her husband's brother was killed in a factory explosion. Her husband had been in the army at one time, so her son joined the army and became a mercenary. He fought in countries where there were civil wars. She wasn't happy about that and wanted him to come home and settle down but he told her nothing was going to happen to him. I think he was taken by aeroplane at sunset and dropped behind the lines but always came home safe and sound. In the end he said he would go on a final mission and then come home for good. He ended up in a reclusive country where the United States wanted to overthrow the government. The government troops attacked and killed the mercenaries; some bodies were shown on television and pictures were published in the papers although it was difficult to identify them. She believed that some had been taken prisoner and her son was one of them."

"I remember that kind of thing happening in that country but wasn't a peace deal signed and all the prisoners released?"

"Yes, it was and prisoners were released but she believed that the country was still holding some prisoners including her son. Did she say anything to you?"

"She said she wanted her son to have everything when he came home but I didn't know about him being killed or taken prisoner. I remember the other witness – he wasn't the one who witnessed Rosie's will – said his grandparents had made their wills. They left everything to each other and then to their children. The solicitor said they ought to include a provision that if anything happened to the children it would go to the grandchildren. He said she ought to include a provision in case anything happened to her son. She said she wanted her son to have everything and leave it at that. He couldn't persuade her at all."

"When you witnessed the will was anything written on it apart from her son having everything."

"No, there wasn't anything."

"Are you sure?"

"Yes, I am. Why?"

"When the will was found after her death we saw she had written that anything happens to her son everything was to go to her husband's brother's two sons. It was squeezed it above and at the side of her signature. It must have been written in later, so it's not valid."

"If the son's dead won't they get it in any case?"

"No, they're not blood relatives."

"What about her brother's family?"

"He wasn't married."

"Who will get it?"

"Descendants of aunts and uncles if there are any, failing that it will go to the Crown."

"Has anything like that happened before with a will?"

"One of the solicitors said that during the war a tail gunner set off on an aerial bombing raid on Berlin. Neither the bomber nor its crew were seen again. The gunner's mother saw a photograph in a Swiss journal which she believed was a picture of her son between two German guards. After the war the Air Ministry certified that for official purposes he was presumed to have lost his life at the time of the raid. Soon afterwards she reluctantly administered her son's estate but still continued to believe he was still alive. She made a will leaving her estate to her son. The court said it was virtually certain the son had died on the bombing raid and it must be presumed to be so."

"What happened to her estate?"

"She included an alternative provision it was to go to charity. I wish Mrs Jones had done that before she signed."

What the second witness had said hadn't made any impact on Mrs Jones at the time but was the kind of matter that lay dormant in the subconscious and surfaced later on but it had been too late.

"Is there anything they can do about it?"

"We'll have to see. This is one of my first jobs and I want to make a success of it."

Jane knew the importance of creating a good impression and understood Mary's concern. Having acted as a witness she was interested to know the outcome and asked Mary to keep her informed. Jane arranged to meet Barbie who also organised activities for local children. Barbie had twelve members in her club whereas Jane had only the three core members. When they met she took her trio with her and they didn't allow themselves to be overawed or intimidated at being outnumbered. Some of Barbie's group were older and one girl had a rough background but Jane suspected she had told them to be considerate. Anyway both sets of children were similar types and had a natural chemistry between them. While they were immersed in their activities Jane and Barbie discussed ideas.

Barbie's club included three sisters and a brother. A friend or relative had made a will and intended to leave a sum of money to each of them but had left out the name of one of the girls.

"How did that happen?" asked Jane.

"I suppose the solicitors left out the name of the sister or she forgot to tell the solicitors."

"Did solicitors draw up the will? The ladies in the home wrote out their own wills."

"Perhaps she wrote out her own will and left out the name. Anyway the others said they would split the three sums of money among four of them. I like to think that attending the club and mixing with other children helps to make them generous. Children who are forced to be on their own can become mean and self centred. That kind of generosity can teach the grown ups something."

Jane had to agree. It also made her think about wills that weren't properly drawn up.

"Was everything all right with the wills you witnessed?"

Jane wished they had not started to talk about the wills. She wanted Mary to be able to trust her and had to avoid betraying her confidence. Anyway the subject of other people's wills was not the kind she wanted to discuss. She had to find an evasive reply.

"They are being dealt with."

"It must have been an interesting experience witnessing a will."

"Yes." Jane wished she had said nothing when Barbie had first mentioned the will. She would have mentioned splitting the money and moved onto something else. She racked her brains for a topic.

"Sometime ago you said a magazine was to be produced and your members had been asked to write something to be included. I had forgotten all about it. What happened?"

"I never heard any more about it; it must have been an idea that came to nothing."

One of the girls came in with a query and the conversation was changed. The meeting was a success and they discussed ideas for the future.

"Do you think Josephine's brother is really a prisoner?" Danielle asked the other two as they were travelling back.

"What's he done?" Jane asked her.

Danielle said that Josephine's brother who was a lot older than she was had become a mercenary. He had been dropped from an aeroplane at sunset into the same country as Mrs Jones' son had been. Not long before the peace deal had been signed he and others in his troop had been ambushed by government forces and killed, but Josephine's father believed that a few, including his son, had been taken prisoner.

"Why does he believe that?"

"A photo of the bodies was taken, sent to the rest of the world and published in the newspapers. He said a few prisoners could be seen in a corner of the photo and one was his son."

Jane hesitated. "Weren't all the prisoners released when the peace deal was signed?"

"They were supposed to be but some weren't."

"How does he know his son was one of the prisoners? If they were in the corner of the photo it wouldn't have been possible to tell who they were."

"He still said one was his son."

"How does he know some weren't released?"

"Because his son wasn't released and later some were seen in a prisoner of war camp."

"Who saw them?"

"She didn't say."

"What is he going to do about it?"

"We don't know."

Should Jane mention it to Mary? There was nothing very definite about what Josephine had told the others. If a government signed a peace deal surely it would keep its word, but could all governments be trusted? If prisoners had been kept wouldn't the rest of the world have realised that by now? She had not arranged any further meetings with Mary and apart from the wills they had nothing in common. Her request to be kept informed was the kind that would be shoved to the back of the drawer. Anyway she would be only relaying some third hand information which children had told her. Yet some time later she ran into Mary in the street and mentioned Josephine's brother.

"You promised you wouldn't discuss this with anyone, least of all with children."

"The children mentioned it without me asking them. Of course I didn't say anything about the wills of Rosie and Mrs Jones."

Mary said what Jane had been thinking and added, "I remember a newspaper report that some prisoners hadn't been released and were held in a prisoner of war camp, but the report wasn't considered to be very reliable. We did discuss the possibility at the office. The Government might have kept prisoners and hidden them from the outside world."

"Why would it do that?"

"Possibly for revenge. They might have carried out some daring raids and caused the government a lot trouble and it wants to get its own back by making sure they are never released. It might have kept them to use for bargaining if there is any further trouble with other countries. It might have not released them by oversight and having said it had released all the prisoners it can't tell the rest of the world it hasn't told the truth. Anyway the odds there are any prisoners must be a hundred to one against. There have been no more press reports and even the most secretive government couldn't keep prisoners hidden forever."

"Yet Mrs Jones believes her son's a prisoner and Josephine's father seems to believe it."

"It must be a question of not being able to accept that someone isn't coming back. One of the solicitors has met cases of children leaving home and not being seen or heard of again. The parents still believe that one day the children will walk in through the door and the family can continue as though nothing happened with things like Sunday lunches, watching favourite television programmes and days out, but things like that can't happen again."

"Has anything happened about the wills?"

"Rosie's son was living at the same address all those years and didn't bother to answer her letters. He complained to the current matron of the home about the solicitors being informed about his mother's death before he was. She said she had met that kind of thing before and it was the case of the son suffering from a guilt complex."

Jane had two similar experiences. Someone had been kind to her family and she wanted to write to her but never found the time. Eventually she did write but the letter was returned marked 'gone away' and she never found out her new address. Another time she wished to apologise for something she had done wrong. She knew she ought to do so but couldn't overcome her embarrassment. Twice she had set off to visit the lady but had turned back. The third time she plucked up enough courage but when she arrived at the house it was devoid of furniture and the garden was overgrown. She asked a neighbour but he had no idea what had happened. If only she had had the sense to visit the lady at the outset any embarrassment would have been over in a matter of minutes.

"What about Rosie's father or can the son claim her estate?"

"The son had never heard anything about his father and it's unlikely he'll come back. Mr Lamb, the probate solicitor said a policy of insurance may be taken out to cover any possible claims by Rosie's husband or the estate may be paid to her son if her signs an agreement to repay the money if his father ever turns up."

"What about Mrs Jones' will and her son being a prisoner?"

"I told the Mr Lamb about what you said about Josephine's brother. He also said it was information supplied third hand by children and there was nothing conclusive about it."

"So what's going to happen?"

"It is virtually certain her son was killed by the government troops and it will be presumed to be so. In the case of the gunner sent on the bombing raid to Berlin no bodies were known to have been seen, but was presumed to have lost his life. In the case of Mrs Jones' son bodies were produced and it is virtually certain he was killed and so death will be presumed. As far as we know she had no aunts or uncles and everything will pass to the Crown, so we'll write to the Treasury Solicitor."

"The death of Josephine's brother would have been presumed as well."

"I suppose so."

"Isn't there anything her husband's brother's family can do? I would have thought they could have made some kind of claim on the estate."

"Someone who had been wholly or partly maintained by a deceased person can make a claim for provision from an estate. Mrs Jones had no contact with the two boys until about eighteen months ago. She started to send them Christmas presents, birthday presents and some summer holiday money. Mr Lamb had to tell their mother that wasn't sufficient to amount to being maintained by Mrs Jones. He tried to tell her as nicely as possible but she has been unemployed and got into debt. He promised to mention the two boys when he wrote to the Treasury Solicitor but she still took it very badly. He's worried she is desperate and may do something stupid."

"How old are the boys?"

"Four and six."

"Where does she live?"

Mary told her the mother's address.

"She lives close to Danielle and I think I know she is. At the club we sometimes do things to help families but I'm not sure what we can do in this case."

Next day Jane met Danielle and asked her about the two boys.

"Some days I see the elder boy going to primary school. Is anything wrong?"

"I know someone who knows the family and was wondering."

"I saw him going to school today."

The following day Mary telephoned Jane to say that the Treasury Solicitor would consider making what was known as an 'ex gratia' payment to the family. "Mr Lamb was going to write to the mother but I said I would go and see her this evening. Do you want to come too?"

"Yes, I do. This could have a happy ending.

On the way they passed Danielle and her mother.

"I know the father was killed and the mother suffers from financial problems and depression; the younger boy's not well," said her mother.

"What's wrong with him?"

"We don't know. She has kept herself to herself since the father's death. The boy always wears a jumper and rarely goes out. When we went past the two boys were standing by the window. We waved and they waved back."

"At least we can tell her she'll get help with her financial problems," said Mary as she rang the bell. The elder boy came to the door.

"May we see your mother?"

"She's lying down."

"Would you tell her we want to see her?"

The boy didn't answer and his brother joined him

"Can we come in?"

The boy seemed uncertain but stood aside. Danielle's mother was right in saying the younger boy wasn't well; he was thin and had a strange complexion. Jane couldn't understand what illness he could have.

"Where is your mother?"

"In the front room."

They entered the room; it was dusty and items were scattered. A woman was lying on the sofa. Jane went up to her and turned round.

"How long has your mother been like this?"

"On Sunday she lay down and didn't get up again."

"Four days ago! What have you two been doing?"

"Going to school. Tommy stayed at home."

"You got yourselves up in the morning and went to school?"

"Yes."

"What did you do about meals?"

"I had school meals and bought things with my pocket money for me and Tommy."

"Didn't you tell your teacher or somebody else?"

"No."

"We'll get someone to look after your mother and someone else to look after you as well. What's your name?"

"Lenny."

Jane hoped she had said the right thing. Mary took the boys into the kitchen. Jane stayed where she was and then called Mary back.

"The mother's a drug addict." Jane pulled up the mother's sleeve and they knew she must have injected herself at some time.

"Oh, Jane! The drugs must have killed her. What are we going to do?"

"We won't know what's killed her until there's been a post mortem. I know someone who works for Social Services. Thank goodness there's a phone in this house; I hope it hasn't been cut off." Jane picked up the receiver. "It's not been cut off."

They returned to the kitchen. The boys couldn't understand their situation. The girls found some tinned food and prepared a meal for them. Lenny was hungry but Tommy didn't have much of an appetite. Jane phoned an undertaker and explained the problem. She contacted a friend who worked for the Social Services to arrange emergency foster care for the boys and for the house to be secured. How could nobody have noticed the boys were caring for themselves? Because the mother kept herself to herself the neighbours didn't bother her. How could she have been feeling as her life was slipping away and the room, the furniture, the pictures and familiar shapes were fading? Did she think about her boys what the future held for them?

"Your jumper's dirty," Mary told Tommy. "We had better find you a clean one."

"Only Mummy puts a jumper on Tommy because he's ill."

"Do you know what's wrong with him?"

"Mummy didn't tell me. She gives him medicine."

"What kind of medicine?"

"I don't know."

"Where does Mummy keep your clean clothes?"

"In the wardrobe upstairs but she's got to put on the clean clothes."

Tommy dropped a piece of food on the floor and bent down to pick it up.

"The child's a drug addict," Jane whispered to Mary. "When he bent down the sleeve of his jumper was pulled up and I saw needle marks."

Mary turned white and raised a hand to her mouth. Jane was attacked by a queasy feeling in her stomach. The sight of Lenny eating exacerbated the feeling.

"What kind of mother would inject her child with drugs?" Mary had to force the words out.

"I don't think any mother would. Their mother may not have been an addict when Lenny was born but became addicted before Tommy was born. He would have been born a drug addict but I'm not sure if he would have lived until now. He must have become an addict because of an awful accident."

They stood in silence waiting for assistance. Tommy must have been a good looking boy but the drugs were destroying his looks; they would also be rotting his organs and he might not survive to be an adult. Even he did his appearance would shock people and he couldn't form a relationship. If he was capable of being employed he would have to be given a job where he was hidden away from people and be assailed by loneliness.

"Tommy couldn't have lasted since Sunday without becoming seriously ill. Somebody must have been giving him a fix." Jane approached Lenny. "Has Tommy been ill in the last two or three days?"

"No, because I've been giving him his medicine."

"Where is his medicine kept?"

"Up there." Lenny pointed to the top shelf of the kitchen cabinet.

"How did you get it?"

"I climbed up."

Jane looked at the top shelf and whispered to Mary, "I think it's cocaine." Then she asked Lenny, "How did Tommy take the medicine?"

"I heard Mummy say it was inhaling."

Jane whispered, "His mother must have sometimes injected him and at other times let him inhale it. If only she had had the sense to get help but she mightn't have wanted the boys to be taken into care."

"They would have been better off in care."

"Have you taken any of the medicine," Jane asked Lenny.

"No, I'm not ill."

The mother may have been fond of her boys but if she had lived how could she have come to terms with herself knowing the kind of life she was preparing for them?

"Jane, I can't stand this any longer; I don't feel well and want to go home."

"All right, you go home. I'll manage on my own."

Lenny could have no idea what he had been giving his little brother and Jane prayed he would never know. He must be of above average intelligence to be able to do what he thought was right to help his little brother and have the sense not to take what he believed to be medicine. Some of the children who attended her activities might be rough and boisterous but they came from homes where drugs were forbidden and they were too sensible to take drugs however much they were pressurised.

The undertakers arrived; Jane ensured the kitchen door was shut and showed them into the front room. The undertaker and his assistant shut themselves in and then removed the body.

"Who was that?" asked Lenny.

"Someone seeing to your mother."

Sometime the boys would have to be told. It would be better for a person experienced in child care to tell them. They would be upset but the person would cause the least possible.

What did the future hold for both Lenny and Tommy? At best a happy foster home where they could enjoy the security of family life, grow up into stable adults and in turn raise a happy family. At worst an orphanage; they were to be avoided but sometimes that was not possible. They would be thrust into a crowd of kids they had never seen before, feel out of place and be unable to settle down; they would be at risk of being assaulted or abused. In adult life they would be incapable of holding down a job or forming a relationship and would turn to drugs or alcohol. Even if he lived to adulthood Tommy would be more at risk having been addicted. Only time would tell.

It might be some time before the impact struck Jane and probably Mary too; both of them would have to cope with it. Mary had set her heart on making a success of the matter and creating a good impression but it had ended in distress. If the will had been professionally prepared or the letter from the Treasury Solicitor had arrived a week earlier all might have ended differently. Yet was Mary in any way to blame? In any event the experience must affect her progress in her job. Jane would support her in any problems with her firm.

The boys were taken into emergency foster care and then removed to a children's home in another area. Jane didn't hear of them again.

SECRET OF THE ROOF

By

Nigel Miller

"Mrs Stevens looks worried," whispered Denise. "She used to live near us but Mr Stevens died and she moved to a smaller house. Mum thought she was happy in her new home."

"Yes, she does look worried," agreed Jane who was with her three young friends.

She went up to Mrs Stevens and greeted her. The three children followed.

"I hope everything is all right in your new home."

"Yes, it is." Mrs Stevens hesitated, "except for one thing."

"Would you like to tell us?"

Mrs Stevens had bought the end terraced house in a row of four; it consisted of two downstairs and two upstairs rooms; it had no front garden and a tiny back garden; it was situated in a pleasant cul-de-sac and was a property and elderly person could manage. The surveyor had reported that it was structurally sound. The solicitors completed the legal work and said everything was in order. Sometimes in the evenings she thought she heard someone creeping around or items being moved under the roof. She had no loft and couldn't imagine what the noises could be. Her next door neighbours were out most of the time. They did tell her it was the timbers creaking but she was sure it wasn't that kind of noise. The third property was empty. The people living in the other end house said they had no problem.

"Perhaps it's rats or mice," suggested Jane. "We had them before we had a cat."

"It doesn't sound like rats or mice."

"I would ask the surveyor."

"I don't think I can; he may say it's nothing to do with the structure."

"Try asking the solicitors."

"They'll say it's not a legal matter."

"Would you like me to come back this evening?"

"Yes, if you would."

"We'll come as well," said Danny.

"I don't think Mrs Stevens would want...."

"No, I don't mind them coming as well."

The four of them went to her house and waited on the landing.

"There isn't any noise." Then Danny added in an undertone, "She's imagined it."

Jane nudged him. "It could happen later."

Soon they heard a sound similar to that of somebody creeping along and shifting an object.

"Perhaps it's ghosts," Danny whispered.

"Don't be so stupid," Jane whispered back. "You're old enough to know better and you'll upset Mrs Stevens." She turned to the old lady. "You're right; it doesn't sound like timbers creaking or like rats."

"I don't know what to do. Perhaps the ceiling will fall down."

"I'm sure nothing like that will happen."

"I'll look round outside." Danny went into the garden and walked all round. He stood in the blackness, a stalker in the night; he stared at the roof and saw nothing. Then he told the others.

"We can check the ceiling for you," Jane offered. "Dad will let me have the steps."

"I'll be grateful if you would."

"You remember she said 'Perhaps the ceiling will fall down.'?" Denise said to the others when they had left. "I remember Daddy saying someone relied on a good report by a surveyor, bought a house and then found the roof was in a dangerous condition. The surveyor hadn't done his job properly and was sued for damages. Perhaps Mrs Stevens' surveyor hasn't done his job properly either and she ought to go and see him."

"Mrs Stevens is right; he'll say it is nothing to do with the structure."

"I'll ask Daddy what to do."

"All right, but first let's check the ceiling."

Next day Jane brought the steps and each of them felt the ceiling in turn.

"Do you hear any noises during the day?"

"Occasionally."

"It seems hollow here."

Jane and Danny tapped around that area.

"It's about the size of a trap door."

"Someone's papered over it," added Danny.

"I'll never rest until I know why it's there, but I don't know what to do. The surveyor and the solicitors won't be interested."

Jane and the children knew the old lady was agitated. The problem would never have disturbed them; it was different for an older person but could they find a solution?

"We could cut away the paper and find out," Danny suggested.

"Mrs Stevens doesn't want her ceiling ruined," said Danielle.

"We can easily put the paper back; I've helped Dad do it at home."

"I don't really know about that." The old lady was weighed down by indecision. She longed to dig to the root of her problem but the process would be an ordeal for her. The four of them glanced at each other. To pressurise her either way would create more anxiety.

"We'll come and see you tomorrow," said Jane.

As they shut the garden gate she called after them and Jane went back.

"As long as you can put the ceiling back I'll be grateful if you'll do that." She hesitated. "There's something else I ought to tell you."

The three children had followed her.

"It's getting late, so you had better go home," Jane told them and they left.

"My situation is rather unusual." She hesitated and Jane didn't press her. "I was married but my husband was killed in a train crash. We were living with his parents while we saved up to buy a house. I had no family of my own and his parents said I could live there as long as I wanted. My husband's brother was also living at home; he was married but his wife died. At least he knew she was dying and had a chance to say 'Goodbye'. We both thought we might remarry but neither of us ever did. I thought I might get a home of my own but never did so and I don't think my parents in law minded.

"After my parents in law died I lived with my brother in law. We were Mr and Mrs but not married. My husband had a sister who left home, married and had a family. She may have been jealous of me but never said anything and was pleasant enough when we met. My parents in law made a will leaving the house to my brother in law which caused some family friction and we didn't see her so often. After my brother in law died I found out he had made a will appointing his solicitor to be the executor and leaving the house to me. I hadn't known about the will and hadn't asked him to make it. Yet my sister in law may have thought he had been pressurised and I rarely see her. I have no family of my own and would love to be in contact with her children.

"I think the people next door may have some connection with her husband but I don't know that for a fact. It did occur to me that they were making those noises on purpose to frighten me but I may be completely wrong."

"Yes, I know; wills can cause problems but people have to make them. Anyway is her husband the type of person who would do that?"

"I didn't think so."

"I'm sure he couldn't have anything to do with it. Don't worry about it and we'll come back tomorrow."

Jane was relieved; she had acted wisely in allowing Mrs Stevens to make up her own mind about investigating the roof. The next day they brought their implements. Danny cut away the paper round the hollow area. He took great care to ensure he caused no more damage than was absolutely necessary. Jane was concerned about what might be revealed and now sensed that Mrs Stevens doubted if she had made the right decision. When he had finished the cutting the others supported the material and laid it on the floor.

"It's only cavity," exclaimed Mrs Stevens.

Danny climbed the steps. "There's a trap door at the top."

"I can't understand it. There was nothing on the estate agents' particulars about a loft and the solicitors said nothing."

Danny pushed. "It can't have been opened for years and has become stuck or somebody's fastened it down."

"Let's try together," he suggested.

"All right," agreed Jane, "but don't do any damage."

The three children arranged themselves at the top of the steps and shoved.

"Don't break your necks!" Mrs Stevens cried out as the steps shook.

The trap door crashed open and they heaved themselves through. Mrs Stevens heard them draw in their breaths and move around. She stood by the bottom rung of the steps with Jane.

"What are you doing up there?" Her voice showed her alarm.

Danielle climbed down. "You mightn't believe this, but your neighbours have got a workshop in their attic and have been using yours as an extension."

"I never thought it could be something like that." It was sometime before the old lady could speak again. "Where are the others?"

"Danny's looking round the house."

"I would rather he didn't; I don't want any trouble with the neighbours."

"Danny! Come back!" Danielle called and he and Denise climbed down. "You didn't touch anything, did you?"

"Of course not!"

"Would you shut the trap door? I don't want them to know we've found out."

"We've shut it as best we can," said Danny. "There's a little space but they probably won't notice."

"I don't know what to do about this; I don't like them moving around above me."

"Why don't you see your solicitors?"

"Will they want to be involved?"

"They'll have to be. If you make an appointment I'll come with you. In the meantime I'll ask Dad about it."

They all sensed Mrs Stevens was far from happy with the situation but would become more agitated at a risk to her health if nothing was done.

"I asked Dad," Jane told the others when they next met. "He said the neighbours have probably got what's known as 'Squatters' rights' and she can't do anything about it, but don't tell her that."

"That means there's no point in her going to her solicitors," said Danielle. "They may charge her and she'll be paying for nothing."

"Yes, I know, but she may take it better if they tell her."

Jane accompanied Mrs Stevens and they explained the problem. The solicitor emitted a long low whistle. "I've never met a case like this before." He shifted through the documents. "The solicitors acting for the vendors never mentioned this when we raised the usual enquiries before contract. The vendors appear to have been a young couple who lived there for less than two years. The previous owners lived there for about eight years but we have no means of knowing if they were aware of it. I don't think the problem about your brother in law's will is relevant; this matter may have begun before he died."

Salina glanced at Mrs Stevens. "Can she get her attic back?"

"If her neighbours have occupied it for twelve years they have 'Squatters' rights'. The problem is that we don't know how long they've done so. However if they've done so in secret they can't claim 'Squatters' rights'."

"Does that mean I can claim the attic?"

"The problem is that they may claim they already had 'Squatters' rights' before the young couple bought your house. The couple might have known nothing about it and not been bothered by the noise. If your neighbours had occupied the attic by agreement they wouldn't have 'Squatters' rights' but we have no means of knowing."

"If they have 'Squatters' rights' does it mean I can't claim the attic?"

"If they move out you can claim it but not otherwise."

"What can I do about it?"

"We can take this matter up with your neighbours but can't guarantee you'll succeed. It's only fair to advise you that this kind of dispute can drag on for ages and end up in court; and whether you win or lose they may make life unpleasant for you."

"I don't want that; I would like to think about it."

"All right, we won't charge you for this interview, but if you want us to act for you it's only fair to warn you we'll have to ask you for some money on account of costs."

"I don't know what to do," Mrs Stevens complained after they had left. "I can't cope with any unpleasantness but I can't live there now. If I sell I suppose I'll have to tell the purchasers and they won't buy it."

"I know that will be a problem."

The children asked Jane about the outcome of the interview; she told them in outline and warned them to keep quiet about it. The children knew how to cope with the problem of another child who might have difficulties at school, at home or with another child which could be resolved; but how could they cure the anguish of an elderly person? The legal talk hadn't diminished her dilemma. She might have to accept she could do nothing about it.

"Let's reclaim the attic!" Danny cried out later.

"We can't unless her neighbours move out," Denise told him. "Weren't you listening to Jane?"

"Of course I was, but we can still do it."

"How?"

"When they're out we'll move their things into their attic and board it up. Dad's got some spare planks and nails."

"I don't think Mrs Stevens wants us to do that," said Danielle.

"I don't think she will," said Jane when she was told, "but we'll see what she says."

"No, I would rather you didn't," Mrs Stevens confirmed.

After the children had taken their leave she called them back.

"If I don't reclaim the attic I'll have to stay there for ever. Would you be able to do it quickly without causing any trouble?"

"Yes, we can," they assured her.

"They are usually out in the daytime but I don't know will happen if they happen to come home while you doing it."

"Don't worry; there'll be four of us."

"They've got a son who is a bit wild. He doesn't live at home but he sometimes calls and some of his friends are a bit wild too."

"I don't want the children to be hurt," said Jane.

"We'll sort him out," Danny assured her.

"He's a lot older than you."

"Danny's granddad taught him boxing," said Danielle. "There are some wild children at school; Danny is able to stand up for himself."

"I can get some other boys to help sort him out," added Danny.

"However I reclaim the attic it will cause unpleasantness. I would like to get it over with. How soon can you do it?

"We can do it tomorrow."

They brought the planks and nails and began to clear the attic.

"You won't damage anything, will you?" Mrs Stevens called out.

"No, we won't," Danielle promised her.

Getting organised and removing the items without damaging them was far more time consuming than any of them had anticipated. Some items were bulky; some were sharp; some were heavy and needed two of them to lift them which was difficult when they had nothing to get hold of. One container was too wide to be passed through the opening: so they had to remove the contents, turn it sideways and replace them; any fool could tell they had been disturbed. They put everything down in the neighbours' workshop or on their landing and had to leave little room to go past. They had no idea what the neighbours might say and decided not to tell Mrs Stevens. The girls had second thoughts at the back of their minds but eventually the attic was empty.

"You can finish it before they get back, can't you?"

"Yes, we can," Jane assured her.

"Perhaps we should have seen the solicitors first." Mrs Stevens' anxiety shrouded her face.

"I don't think they would want to be involved."

All of them knew Mrs Stevens had been having second thoughts but they hadn't wanted to abandon the task and be laboured with reinstating the attic. Anyway she might change her mind again later. They fitted the planks and Danny banged in the nails.

"They can't get in now."

"Oh dear! Your clothes are dirty and you've got grazes." Mrs Stevens viewed their arms and legs and they dusted down their cotton tee shirts and cord shorts.

"We don't mind," Danny told her.

"They haven't cleaned the attic for years," Danielle complained. "As they were using somebody else's they should have had the decency to keep it clean."

"I hope I've done the right thing and there won't be a lot of trouble."

"If there is we'll sort them out," Danny reassured her.

"Dad won't mind if I sleep here," added Jane.

"I would rather nobody else knew about this."

"Don't worry; you can trust us not to say anything."

In the evening the children returned. They heard somebody moving about in the adjoining attic, knocking on the planks and arguing with someone else. Then all became quiet.

"If they were going to come round and complain they would have done so by now," said Denise.

"We're sure everything will be all right now," added Danielle.

As they left the girls eyed each other. Had Danny's plan of action been crazy? He relished excitement and the idea of doing something wrong motivated him. Should the others have stamped on it at once? Or had they achieved in one day what the legal process might never have accomplished in a year?

Next day the Jane met the children.

"We've just met the neighbour's son and his friends," Danny told her. "He asked us if we were the kids who had been messing about in the attic. We said we were. He said we were asking to be carved up. We told him not to make any trouble or we will sort him out and get some other boys to help. He just walked off and his friends followed him: so we don't think he'll do anything."

"I do hope you're right," said Salina.

A few days later the girls met Mrs Stevens.

"I've met the neighbours several times and they haven't mentioned the attic. It's almost as though they were expecting me to reclaim it."

THE YOUNG WITNESSES

By

Nigel Miller

"It's foggy!" Danielle stopped as they were leaving the building.

Jane had taken her three young friends on an activity. It had been misty when they travelled there and the children amused themselves by noticing how quickly everything disappeared from view. Now it was difficult to see across the street.

"It's probably thicker here," Jane assured her.

They set off in the car and the children looked ahead. When they joined the motorway the fog was thicker still and it was getting dark. Jane dropped her speed but several vehicles overtook her.

"Mummy will be worried if I'm late home," said Danielle.

"Yes, I know but I'm sure she'll understand that it's because of the fog and she would rather you came home in one piece."

"Look at that!" Danielle pointed to a lorry that sped past.

"It's crazy driving at that speed in the fog."

Now fewer vehicles were passing them; that may have been because more drivers were watching their speed or because not so many were venturing onto the motorway. Either way Jane was relieved as fast moving traffic in the fog unnerved her. All the same she wanted to ensure the children arrived at their homes safe and sound as soon as possible and then go home herself.

"They're crazy," Denise pointed at a car that rushed past.

The occupants jeered at them, "Come along, slow coaches!"

"I wish we could catch them up and tell them to come along," said Danny.

"If they have to be stupid let them," Jane told him.

She came behind a vehicle that was crawling along. She agreed that nobody should speed in the fog but why did they have to drive so slowly? They were a hazard and forcing other drivers to move into the outer lanes which could cause danger. She checked her mirror, prayed that no lunatic would be racing towards her and overtook a land rover pulling a trailer.

"Danny! Don't!" She thought he was about to jeer at the occupants.

"I wasn't going to do anything."

"When will we be home?" asked Danielle.

"It's difficult to say but we should be home in an hour."

Now Jane's priority was to reassure the children as anxiety was showing on their faces and they were unnaturally silent. They were past the age of playing 'I spy with my little eye' and old enough to know the perils of fog on the motorway. They had already discussed the activity and she had to find another topic.

"Danny, Peter's dad said he was going to take you and the other boys to the Isle of Man. Did you hear anything more about it?"

"No, I didn't. I think there was a problem about the place where we were going to stay."

"What a pity! I had been planning to go there with some friends but nothing came of it. They say it's worth a visit."

"Dad said we might go there," said Denise. "He was going...."

"Jane! Look out!"

She stamped on the brake. She was going to crash into the back of a vehicle with an object sticking out of the rear. Crack! She avoided crashing but the object poked through the windscreen. It was a few seconds before they were able to realise what had happened. Then they heard the screech of brakes; the lights of a large vehicle were approaching from behind. This time the children were too shocked to call out. They had to hope it wouldn't crash into the car too violently. It seemed to be touching it but it had stopped and they sighed with relief. A high sided lorry stopped in the middle lane next to the vehicle in front and partly alongside the car.

A minute later Jane was able to take in what had happened. A pole with a red cloth attached to the end protruded from the door of the van; it had been firmly secured for it had not been dislodged by the impact. The van had gone into the back of a lorry and beyond the lorry must be the site of the accident.

"Are you all right?" A man had got out of the vehicle behind.

Were they all right? Jane had a few puncture cuts on her face, hands and legs but nothing much. Danny was nearer the object and had a few more cuts on his face and legs. They brushed fragments of glass off their cord shorts and legs.

"Danny, are you all right?"

He was silent for a moment and then replied, "Yes." He wasn't the type of boy to make a fuss.

Jane looked round; she was glad the girls in the back had escaped physical injury.

"Are you all right?"

"Yes," they whispered.

"Yes, we're more or less all right."

"I've got to go and help; I think there are people trapped." He ran off with a first aid box.

People trapped! It now hit Jane that she was in the nightmare of a motorway pile up. She had read about them and heard about them on the news. A police officer or someone else involved would describe what had happened and pictures of damaged vehicles would be shown. However the horror was never brought home to her. Now she was part of it and it seemed unreal.

She had received some training in nursing. Ought she to go and help the injured? She remembered somebody who criticised those who refused to go to help accident victims. Someone else had said you shouldn't stop unless you knew about first aid and were capable of helping, or you would just be in the way. She was torn between two choices. She couldn't bring herself to go. The training she had received wasn't the kind that was any use for motorway accidents and she would be in the way. Anyway should she leave the children? They weren't talking and now shock must have made them silent.

All they could do was to sit there until the emergency services arrived through the fog, the injured were treated and the carriageway was cleared. She heard screeches of brakes, other vehicles coming to a halt and possibly there were some bumps and scrapes. Then she would have to phone for the windscreen to be replaced. A few people ran past her car to help but most stood back.

She knew how people reacted in frustration to the delays. They might drive their car onto the grass verge, leave it there, go home by other means and go back for the car later. They might try to drive across adjoining land to find a way of going home. Even more foolhardy was to cross the central reservation to drive along the outer lane of the other carriageway to bypass the accident, or to do a U turn. The wait might generate frustration in the children and they would pressurise her to take any risk to get them home. She would refuse to do anything crazy but have to find a way of calming them.

"Does anyone know anything about wills?" A man had run back.

"Wills?" queried another man.

"A man who's trapped says he's got to make a will."

Those standing back looked at each other but nobody knew anything about wills. Jane's friend, Mary, was articled to a solicitor and had mentioned wills. Jane had been sent a copy of a will in which was a beneficiary. Could she help?

"I know it bit." She opened the car door.

"Good." The man set off.

Jane turned cold. What had she agreed to do? She couldn't face the prospect of coming face to face with injured and dying people but could she get back in her car? The man stopped by the van in front. She saw that it had crashed into the back of a lorry that hid the rest of the pile up.

"He can talk rationally but to speak to him you'll have to go between the van and that lorry. I'll have to leave you as I've got to help the others." He ran off.

The section of the motorway wasn't lit and the space between the van and the high sided lorry was in darkness. She had expected the man to accompany her and the prospect of speaking to the trapped man on her own in the gloom unnerved her. She had no idea what to expect but crept to the front of the van. He must have been driving too fast for the bonnet was crumpled and the windscreen was close to the back of the lorry. She couldn't make out his features.

"They won't get me out of here. I want everything to go to my stepchildren. If I don't make a will my brother and sister will get it and I don't want that. Please, I've got to make the will."

Jane nearly said, "Don't worry, they'll get you out." but thought "How am I going to do it?"

"I've got my notebook in the car; I'll get it."

"Please be quick; I haven't got long."

She hurried back to the car and grabbed her notebook. She was half way back when she recalled Mary had said that two witnesses were required to a will. She could be one but what about the other? She ran to the people standing back and explained her problem.

"No! We're not going over there." A man turned away.

"Please! He doesn't think he's got long."

"That's nothing to do with us," said a woman.

"Why didn't he make a will before?" demanded another woman.

"Please! Someone's got to come."

"We haven't got to."

"We don't have to be told what to do by tarted up teenagers."

The group moved off. Jane went to the off side of her car and looked round. Nearby was a car with a couple in it. She approached and saw they were elderly but told them what she wanted.

"We would like to help but we're not in good health," said the man. "The doctor has told us not avoid anything that may cause stress or anxiety."

"I am going to have to take a tablet," said the lady.

"All right." She went up to the car behind with a middle aged couple in it.

"We're not getting out of the car and walking on the motorway," snapped the man. "Do you think we're crazy?"

"You must be crazy walking on the motorway half naked," shrieked the woman.

Jane uttered an expletive and could tell the couple heard her. It was hopeless trying to find a witness. She returned to her car and looked towards the van. She couldn't go to the sight of the accident and expect a helper to come. By now the trapped man must be thinking she wasn't coming back. She would have to tell him she couldn't find another witness. It might have been nothing to do with those other people but it hadn't been anything to do with her either. His stepchildren would never get the money but she had done all she could. She had no idea how to tell him. She started to go back and then stopped.

"Danny!" She opened the car door. "Would you please come and witness the will?"

"What? Of the man who's trapped?"

"You know I wouldn't ask you do anything unless I had to."

Danny moved across the driver's seat and got out of the car. She led him along the side of the van. She couldn't make up her mind whether she was doing the right thing or not. In the distance they heard sirens.

He halted. "What have I got to do?"

"I will write out the will, the man will sign it and then we'll sign it."

She led him on.

"I'm glad you're back; I thought you weren't coming." The driver's voice was weaker.

"I'm sorry but I had trouble in finding a second witness."

Some emergency vehicles were driven along the hard shoulder.

"I'm Stephen Waterhouse, spelled with p h."

Jane didn't know how to start to prepare the will. Where could she put her notebook? She found a piece of metal that was firm enough but she couldn't see well enough to write.

"Danny, have you got your torch?"

"Yes, but the battery's getting low."

He shone it on the paper. She tried to keep it as still as she could and wrote, "This is the will of Stephen Waterhouse."

"A will needs executors; they are Albert and Sarah Kingdom."

Jane remembered a clause about appointment of executors but not the wording. She wrote, "Albert and Sarah Kingdom are the executors."

"I want everything to go to my stepchildren, Simon and Susan Banks."

She didn't remember the wording of the clause for the beneficiaries but thought it contained the words "estate" and "property". She wrote, "I give my estate and property." The will she had seen included many extra words but recalling what they were was impossible. She would have to continue, "to Simon and Susan Banks."

"My solicitors are Grant Bayley."

Jane was trying to keep her hand steady.

"I'm very grateful to you. When my wife died the last thing she said was to look after Simon and Susan and I said I would."

"I'm sure you have."

"They telephoned to say Susan wasn't well in school. I was delayed at the delivery point and wanted to get home quickly. I didn't realise how fast I was driving."

"I was also going too fast."

"They'll be all right with Albert and Sarah." The driver's voice was fading.

Jane had written down, "My solicitors are Grant Bayley." and "signed by the testator and witnesses." She was sure the will ought to contain further wording but remembering it was hopeless.

"I've written it out now." How could she get him to sign it? Danny lifted his torch. The driver's face was thrust against the windscreen. It was barely visible but showed his condition was deteriorating. His right arm was free but she had no notion of the state of the rest of his body crushed between the might of metal. She held up her notebook and rested it against the door. Then she handed him her pen. He could only turn his head a fraction but he took it. He wrote on the bottom of the sheet of paper and the pen fell. She lowered her notebook. The signature consisted of a shaky S and W, a half formed t, a squiggle, a half formed h and a slanting line. Should she find her pen and hold up the notebook again so he could complete his signature?

"Can you see the pen?"

Danny shone the torch on the ground; the pen was at her feet and she picked it up. She placed the notebook on a piece of metal and signed "Jane Carberry" as firmly as she could. Then she handed the pen to Danny and he signed "Danny Hartland" as clearly as he could in the circumstances.

"It's done."

More emergency vehicles were arriving. Someone on the hard shoulder shone a torch at the driver's cabin and walked off. Jane thought the driver said something.

"I'll make sure your solicitors get your will."

Someone was standing near the space between the vehicles; he turned to speak to somebody else.

"I will make sure your solicitors get your will."

"He didn't answer." Danny shone the torch. The driver's head was resting near the van door and his hand was hanging loose. He seemed peaceful.

"Is he dead?"

"I don't know."

Danny lowered the torch. "What's that? It's blood."

Blood had trickled from underneath the lorry in front and formed a pool. A car had been shoved underneath. It must have contained those who jeered. What chance did flesh have squeezed under heavy metal? They would have suffered a few second agony and then oblivion.

"Is that a bit of a person?" The torch lit up something protruding from under the lorry.

Jane took Danny's hand. "We'll go back to the car. They're coming to attend to him." Some people were about to enter the space and she led him towards the car.

"Jane, I feel cold."

"Yes, I know." She felt cold too. "Don't tell Danielle and Denise about the driver or the blood."

"No, I won't."

He walked round the car to get to the passenger's door and a police car went past.

"Get out of the way!" an officer shouted. "It's dangerous to walk around on the motorway."

"He didn't have to shout."

"No, he didn't but don't worry about it."

"We thought something had happened to you and you weren't coming back," said Danielle. "We didn't know what to do...."

"Yes, I sorry about that but we couldn't help it."

"A man shone a torch at the driver's seat," said Denise.

"He was probably checking to see if anyone was hurt."

Danny was white faced and he raised his hand to his mouth as if he might be sick. The girls didn't ask what had happened but their faces revealed their upset at waiting on their own. Jane wanted put her head on the wheel and shut herself out. She felt incapable of driving but her priority was to take the children to their homes as soon as she could. When no more emergency vehicles were arriving she must phone for a windscreen replacement. When it had been replaced and the motorway was reopened she would have to drive. Ambulances were being driven away.

"I am going to the nearest phone. Do you want to stay here or come with me?"

"We'll come with you."

They got out of the car and ran to the far edge of the hard shoulder. The three children hugged each other. Danny gave Jane a hug and the girls followed suit and they were reassured. They didn't have to pass the accident to reach the nearest phone. Various vehicles were parked there but they couldn't see what was happening. On the way they overheard someone grumbling about being delayed. Someone else was using the phone but when he saw them he finished. Jane explained the details of their situation to the firm.

"If we come now we'll have to park on the hard shoulder which will mean that police cars and ambulances can get past."

"I think they've all come."

"You can't be sure. If we block their way we could be in trouble. Another thing – we can't replace your windscreen until you can back your car."

Jane accepted the situation and had to tell the children. They were in danger of panicking about what their parents would think. She contacted the control centre and they agreed to phone the parents. Again they hugged each other.

"We'll go back to the car; it's safer than the hard shoulder."

Most people were sitting in their vehicles. Jane wanted to tell those who refused to be a witness that she had to ask young Danny to do so, she was disgusted with them and they ought to be ashamed of themselves. She also wanted to tell the police officer who shouted at Danny. In her state she couldn't make much impression and they would shout back at her.

Back in the car a sense of shock and frustration overwhelmed them. It was a question of waiting for the motorway to be cleared but heaven alone knew how long it would take. The children fidgeted and all Jane could do was to ask them to be patient. That had a temporary effect.

The high sided lorry was moved and emergency vehicles were stationed by the van. They couldn't make out what was happening but somebody may have been using cutting gear. How did the staff managed to steel themselves to recover the mangled bodies? At least it was a step towards opening the carriageway but how much longer it would be? The outside lane was reopened sooner than Jane had expected. Traffic started to move but the lorry behind them remained where it was.

"I'll see if it can be moved." She got out and walked forward not looking at the van. Some people were standing by the cab of the lorry in front. A few turned round as she approached.

"Don't come over here," snapped a policeman.

"I want to move my car but a lorry is parked behind it. That's why I've come over here."

"That's mine; I'll back it," Jane was relieved to hear the driver say. He backed it at once and left plenty of room for another vehicle to park.

"Were there many casualties?" She ventured to ask.

"Five people were hurt in the original accident but not seriously; some people suffered from shock. Four people were killed when a car went into the back of a lorry at high speed. A van driver was killed when he drove into the back as well."

He confirmed what she had suspected. She phoned the windscreen replacement firm who promised to come at once. They returned to sit in the car. Another policeman approached and she told him how the windscreen was damaged.

"You shouldn't drive so fast in the fog."

"Yes, I know but police officers shouldn't shout at children."

"Sometimes they have to." The officer paused. "Were any of you hurt?"

"Not really, only a few minor cuts."

The officer looked at Danny. "He seems to be suffering from shock and possibly some injuries. He ought to go to hospital for a check up."

"I don't want to go to hospital; I want to go home."

"The best thing to do is to take him home. Anyway being shouted at didn't help."

"I'm sorry about that. If he does show any sign of severe shock or injury get medical help."

Someone from the firm soon arrived, a new windscreen was fitted and they were ready to leave. The motorway wasn't busy at that time of night but a tail back of traffic had formed and Jane couldn't find a gap.

"Surely someone could stop." She couldn't hide her shock and impatience.

At length a lorry driver stopped to let her out and they all gave him a hand signal. The emergency vehicles were still stationed beside the van but the traffic was able to squeeze past. The police must have been prepared to open the outside lane even though the bodies had not been freed. Any ghouls who wanted to stare couldn't catch a glimpse of what was happening.

Jane wanted to avoid having to drive but had to do so. She drove slowly and irritated some other drivers. Most of the time the children were still silent through the shock of the accident and she felt the same. She thanked heaven Danny wasn't in need of medical help and had been resilient enough not to cry, throw up or do both. She succeeded in delivered the children to their homes and received a hug for it.

That night she endured brief periods of fitful sleep. All the time she saw herself driving her car into the back of the van, the driver's life ebbing from him and the pool of blood by the lorry. The driver had been pressurised by his stepdaughter's illness which had made him drive too fast. The driver's injuries must have been so horrendous that he was no longer capable of feeling pain and it was surprising he had survived as long as he did until he could sign his will. She had been guilty of driving fast too. After she had overtaken the land rover and trailer she hadn't slowed down enough. Instead of chatting to the children she should have concentrated on driving in the fog. It was only by luck that her car hadn't ended up beneath the van. She would never have forgiven herself if the children had been killed and she had survived. While she was arranging activities for them they were in her care.

Had she acted sensibly in asking Danny to witness the will? He would have done so under a sense of loyalty. How would she have felt if she had allowed the driver to die without providing for his stepchildren? He would have felt he had broken his promise and let his wife down. However was the will valid?

In the morning she had black rings round her eyes. She had to take the will to the solicitors, Grant Bayley. She would have given anything not to drive but the journey by public transport was difficult and she felt obligated to make it. On the way she ran into dense traffic. Heavy lorries being driven alongside her made her nervous. She was shown into an office of a Mr Richards and did her best to explain the circumstances to an assistant who made notes.

"You asked a young boy to be a witness?"

"I couldn't help it. Is the will all right?"

"I shall have to discuss this with the probate solicitor when he gets back, but I think you did very well with the will. I don't think I could have done it."

Despite the assistant trying to reassure her Jane got the impression she considered the will was no good. Nevertheless she must go round to see that the children were all right even though it involved more driving which she wanted to avoid. She went to Danielle's house first.

"She found the pole going through the window a fright," said her mother, "and she's tired but I think she'll be all right in a few days. We know you weren't to blame."

Danielle came up; she looked tired and under the weather. Yet she seemed please to see Jane and gave her a hug. She went to Denise's house and they said much the same. Danny's family might be a problem and she visited them last.

"Danny's suffering from delayed shock," his father told her. "You must have been driving too fast in the fog."

"I may have been driving a bit fast but I wanted to get them home."

"I can't believe anyone would ask a young boy to witness a will, especially in those circumstances. What on earth could you have been thinking of?"

"We appreciate what you're doing for local children," said his mother, "arranging activities for them and what you did for Danny in the past. We thought we could trust you but now we've got second thoughts."

Jane tried to explain the problem she had in persuading anyone else to be a witness.

"You must have been able to get an adult to be a witness."

She wanted to tell them it was all very well telling her that she must have been able but the truth of the matter was that she couldn't.

"If you had to get Danny to be a witness you could have taken it back to the car for him to sign or when you brought him back one of us could have signed. Anyway the police must have arrived and an officer could have been a witness."

Jane hadn't thought of those possibilities but she would have had to go to the scene of the main accident and the police might have said it wasn't a matter for them.

"Anyway the will isn't valid."

"Why not?"

"It wasn't done on proper will paper. The man didn't sign it properly; Danny told us what the signature was like. He's under 18 and couldn't be a witness. You made him see a man die and a lot of blood and upset him for nothing."

"I'm sorry, but I didn't know about the blood until afterwards and at the time I couldn't think what else to do. It wasn't pleasant for me either."

Danny came out of a room; he was bleary eyed and looked under the weather. "Oh, Mum! Dad! It wasn't Jane's fault." He hugged her but his parents may not have approved.

"All right, we'll let Danny get over it."

Danny said he would see her at the next meeting and she decided she ought to leave. She may have allowed herself to be upset too easily by the couple in the car; if she had gone on to ask other drivers one of them would have been prepared to be a witness. She had created trauma for him and may have achieved nothing.

She hoped he would be allowed to come to the next meeting. She enjoyed putting on activities for local children but she had a problem with numbers: some children weren't interested; some said the activities were boring; some were afraid to go out at night; and some parents were frightened to let their children go on the streets. She hoped the accident wouldn't result in anyone not coming. Danny escorted Danielle and Denise. He was resilient enough to recover from the trauma but if his parents stopped him attending the girls wouldn't be there either. Sometimes other children came but they formed the core membership and that would be the end of the activities.

In the meantime she must find out as much as she could about wills. At the back of her mind had been doubts but Danny's parents had convinced her all the upset had been for nothing. Nevertheless she went to see Mary.

"Did you really get a young boy to witness a will? You must have been able to find someone."

"That's what Danny's parents said but nobody would come and I had to do something."

"I don't know about the will; I'll have to ask a solicitor."

For the present Jane could do no more. On the face of things when the injured and the dead had been taken away, the vehicles had been removed, the blood had been washed away and the carriageway had been repaired the accident was over and done with. That was far from the truth. The pole being shoved through the windscreen, the life of the trapped driver ebbing away and the pool of blood flashed back to her; they would flash back more so to Danny. The two girls would also suffer nightmares. If only the will was valid it would be a matter for relief.

"I have asked a solicitor. A will does not have to be written out on will paper and can be written on note paper. The signature should be accepted by the probate registry. In one case a testatrix who was dying only got half way through her signature and it was accepted as it was intended to be a signature. The Wills Act says there have to be two witnesses but does not say they have to attain the age of majority. However the view is that a person whose faculties are limited or a young child can't be a witness. There is no known reported case about a will being challenged because it was witnessed by a child. How intelligent is Danny and did he know he was being a witness?"

"He's of average intelligence and he did know."

"It would have been no good if you had taken the will back to the car to get Danny to sign or got someone to sign it later as the witnesses have to sign in the presence of the testator. Did you both see him sign and then did he see you both sign?"

Jane hesitated. She had seen the driver sign but had Danny? She hadn't paid any attention to what he was doing but he must have been looking. Had the driver seen then sign? Was he still capable of looking at them? It was possible he had seen them. She had to take a risk. "Yes, he did." The piece of metal on which she had placed her notebook was in front of the windscreen. It was more likely he had seen them than he hadn't. Raking this over in her mind brought back the sight of the driver dying and the pool of blood. She never wanted to drive again.

"The will should have had what is known as an attestation clause to say that the testator knew and approved of the contents, he signed it in the presence of you and Danny and you both signed in his presence. Of course you couldn't have known that. However the will may be accepted if you can swear an oath to that effect. Can you do so?"

"Yes." Jane could cope with that.

"If anyone challenged the validity of the will and there was a court hearing would you be prepared to attend?"

"Yes." She wanted to avoid attending but felt a sense of obligation. "What about Danny?"

"Oh, I don't know what he would have to do, but it's sufficient for one witness to swear an oath." Jane decided not to mention it to him; she couldn't face more problems with his parents.

"One of the clerks said there were some things you could have done although they wouldn't have been legal. You could have written the signature of a fictitious person and said it was someone you had asked to be a witness but didn't who the person was. There was the case of a will with the signature of the testatrix and two witnesses nobody had ever heard of; they couldn't be traced. The court presumed the will had been properly executed. It was possible she invented the people and wrote the signatures herself. You could have said Danny was a grown up who agreed to be a witness but you didn't know his address or who he was."

"They can tell it's a child's writing."

"Some grown ups do have childish writing. You could have asked a grown up to sign later if he was prepared to do so and say you didn't who he was either. The clerk did say that he wasn't suggesting you should have done any of those things, but they could have meant the will would be accepted and the stepchildren would be all right. On the other hand if someone had seen there weren't two witnesses it would have made it worse."

Jane hated the possibility that the stepchildren wouldn't inherit yet she said, "I didn't like having to get Danny to sign but it's better to be legal."

She prepared for the next meeting but wouldn't have been surprised if nobody turned up. However Danny's mother brought him and the two girls. The trio had always come on their own and she had no idea what to expect.

"Danny wants to come. We thought it would do him good and help him get over what happened. We've talked it over and realised you were in an impossible situation. Older people don't want to do what a teenager asks them and can have doubts. If you had been older or dressed more formally they might have been more willing. You couldn't have done anything about that and if you hadn't made the will you might regret it now."

"I'm glad he's looking better. I know he's the type of boy who would do things even if it was unpleasant for him."

She was relieved Danny's parents now appreciated her predicament. The couple in the car and the police office may have had a point about people not walking around on the motorway; they could be a danger to themselves and others. However they could have been more pleasant about it. If she had persevered and found a witness it might have been too late.

The three children continued to attend the meetings. On one occasion the girls said they hoped they would never have to be in a car on their own on a motorway again. Danny said he had a dream about the bit of a person under the lorry.

"I couldn't get back to sleep for ages but I've got over it."

The very fact they were taking part in the activities should focus their minds on pleasanter things and help them to get over the incident; Jane also found it reassuring.

The solicitors, Grant Bayley, wrote to her and asked her to swear an oath in the form Mary had told her. The brother and sister of Mr Waterhouse had previously said the will wasn't valid and they would take proceedings but hadn't taken the matter any further. Remembering what Danny's mother had said she dressed in a more formal outfit and swore before a commissioner for oaths that the will was properly executed. Yet she was racked by doubts. Was it absolutely true to say that all three had signed in each other's presence? Mr Waterhouse was trapped dying in the cab and the will was lower down on the metal. She might have sworn to something that wasn't strictly legal. The solicitors must know the law and the three of them must have been sufficiently in the line of sight.

The solicitors hadn't mentioned Danny apart from referring to him as the other witness. Had they assumed he was over the age of 18? Or had they suspected he was a young boy but making enquiries would have stirred up trouble? They did tell her Mr and Mrs Kingdom were very grateful to her and said it must have taken a lot of courage for her to write the will and witness it and for the other witness too. The interests of the stepchildren had been of paramount importance. They would be distressed by the death of their stepfather but would be cared for by Albert and Sarah Kingdom and be financially secure.

By now the vehicles had been long ago removed, the blood washed away and the carriageway repaired. Jane drove again but never along that part of the motorway with the children. The trauma might fade but the stain would never be erased from their memory.

Other short stories written by this author
Bus ride to hell, Was Danny there?, and Suspicion fell on him
Frighteners in the street
She needed them
The confrontation
The hour of vengeance
The vast unknown, Terror in the trees, The infernal packet, The way to the void and Children of the narrow boat

www.ingramcontent.com/pod-product-compliance
Lightning Source LLC
Chambersburg PA
CBHW050426180526
45159CB00005B/2429